Mérope
Voltaire
Translation by William F. Fleming

Start Publishing PD LLC
Copyright © 2024 by Start Publishing PD LLC

All rights reserved, including the right to reproduce this book or portions thereof in any form whatsoever.

Start Publishing PD is a registered trademark of Start Publishing PD LLC
Manufactured in the United States of America

Cover art: Shutterstock/Taisiya Kozorez

Cover design: Jennifer Do

10 9 8 7 6 5 4 3 2 1

ISBN 979-8-8809-0820-2

Contents

Dramatis PersonÆ.. 3

A Letter to the Marquis Scipio Maffei, Author of the Italian Mérope, and Many Other Celebrated Performances. 4

A Letter From M. de la Lindelle to M. De Voltaire.. 14

The Answer of M. De Voltaire to M. de la Lindelle. 17

Act I. . . . .

Act II. . . . .

Act III. . . . .

Act IV. . . . .

Act V. . . . .

Dramatis Personæ

Mérope, Widow of Cresphontes, King of Messene.
Ægisthus, Son of Mérope.
Poliphontes, Tyrant of Messene.
Narbas, an old Man.
Euricles, Favorite of Mérope.
Erox, Favorite of Poliphontes.
Ismenia, Confidante of Mérope.

"Mérope," produced in 1743, is the greatest of Voltaire's tragedies and a perfect literary performance. Frederick the Great amused himself by turning it into the libretto of an opera. Its success was great and the author was called before the curtain, an honor until then unknown in France. The interest of the following correspondence justifies its length.

A Letter to the Marquis Scipio Maffei, Author of the Italian Mérope, and many other celebrated performances.

Sir:

The Greeks and Romans, to whom modern Italy, as well as all other nations, are indebted for almost everything, dedicated their works, without the ridiculous form of compliments, to their friends, who were masters of the art: by this claim I take the liberty of addressing to you the French "Mérope."

The Italians, who have been the restorers of almost all the fine arts, and the inventors of many, were the first, who, under the auspices of Leo X., revived tragedy; and you, sir, are the first who, in this age, when the Sophoclean art became enervated by love-intrigues, often foreign to the subject, and so often debased by idle buffooneries, that reflected dishonor on the taste of your ingenious countrymen, you, sir, were the first who had courage and genius enough to hazard a tragedy without gallantry, a tragedy worthy of Athens in its glory; wherein the maternal affection constitutes the whole intrigue, and the most tender interest arises from the purest virtue. France prides herself in her "Athalie"; it is indeed the masterpiece of our stage, perhaps of poetry itself: of all the pieces that are exhibited among us, it is the only one where love is not introduced: but at the same time we must allow, that it is supported by the pomp of religion, and that majesty of eloquence which appears in the prophets. You had not that resource, and yet you have so contrived, as to furnish out five acts, which it is so extremely difficult to fill up without episodes. I must own, your subject appeared to me much more interesting and tragical than that of "Athalie"; and even if our admirable Racine had worked up his masterpiece with more art, more poetry, and more sublimity than he has, yours, I am satisfied, would have drawn more tears from the audience.

The preceptor of Alexander—kings ought always to have such preceptors—the great Aristotle, that extensive genius, so just, and so deeply versed in all the learning of those times, Aristotle, in his art of poetry, has declared that the meeting of Mérope and her son was the most interesting circumstance of the whole Grecian theatre. This stroke was, in his opinion, infinitely superior to all the rest. Plutarch tells us, that the Greeks, who, of all the people in the world, had the quickest feeling, trembled with fear, lest the old man who was to stop the arm of Mérope, should not come in time enough. That piece, which was played in his time, and a few fragments of which are still extant, appeared to him the most affecting of all the tragedies of Euripides; but it was not the choice of his subject alone to which that poet owed his success, though in every species of the drama, a happy choice is, no doubt, of the greatest service.

France has seen several "Méropes," but none of them ever succeeded: the authors perhaps overloaded this simple subject with foreign ornaments: it was the naked "Venus" of Praxiteles which they wanted to cover with tinsel. It requires a great deal of time to teach men that everything which is great should be simple and natural. In 1641, when the French flag began to flourish, and even to raise itself above that of Greece, by the genius of P. Corneille, Cardinal Richelieu, who ambitiously sought for glory of every kind, and who had just then built a magnificent hall, for theatrical representations, in the Palais Royal, of which he had himself furnished the design, had a "Mérope" played there under the name of "Telephonte"; the plot of it is generally believed to have been entirely his own. There are about a hundred verses in it, supposed to be written by him; the rest was by Colletet, Bois-Roberts, Desmarets, and Chapelain; but all the power of Cardinal Richelieu could not impart to those writers that genius which they never possessed: his own was not indeed adapted to the stage, though he had a good taste; so that all he could do, or that could be expected from him, was to patronize and encourage the great Corneille.

Mr. Gilbert, resident of the celebrated Queen Christina, in 1643, gave us his "Mérope," which is at present as little known as the other. La Chapelle, of the French academy, author of a tragedy called "Cléopatre," which was played with some success, gave us another "Mérope" in 1683, and took care to insert a love episode: he complains withal in his preface, that the critics reproached him with too great a degree of the marvellous; but he was mistaken, it was not the marvellous that sank his performance, but in reality the want of genius, added to the coldness and insipidity of his versification; this is the great point, the capital fault, that condemns so many poems to oblivion.

The art of eloquence in verse is of all arts the most difficult and the most uncommon: there are a thousand geniuses to be found who can plan a work, and put it into verse after the common manner; but to treat it like a true poet, is a talent which is seldom bestowed on above two or three men on the face of the whole earth.

In December, 1701, M. de la Grange played his "Amasis," which is nothing more than the subject of "Mérope" under another name. Gallantry has its share in this performance likewise; and there is more of the marvellous in it than even in La Chapelle's: but it is more interesting, conducted with more art and genius, and written with more warmth and power; notwithstanding which, it met with no great success;

Et habent sua fata libelli.

Since that, however, it has been revived with great applause; and is one of those few pieces which generally give pleasure in the representation.

Before and after "Amasis" we have had several tragedies on subjects very nearly resembling this, wherein a mother is going to avenge the death of her son on the son himself, and discovers him just at the instant when she was about to kill him. We frequently saw on our stage that striking but rarely probable situation, wherein a person comes with a poniard in his hand ready to destroy his enemy, and another arrives at the same instant, and snatches it from him. This incident recommended, at least for a time, the "Camma" of Thomas Corneille.

But amongst all the tragedies on this subject, which I have here enumerated, there is not one of them but is filled with some episode of love, or rather gallantry; for everything must give way to the reigning taste. But you must not believe, sir, that this unhappy custom of loading our tragedies with ridiculous love-intrigues was owing to Racine; a crime, which, in Italy, I know he is generally reproached with: on the contrary, he did everything in his power to reform the public taste in this particular: the passion of love is never brought in by him as a mere episode; it is the foundation or ground-plot of all his pieces, and forms the principal interest: it is certainly of all the passions the most truly theatrical, the most fruitful in sentiments, and admits of the greatest variety: it ought, therefore, no doubt, to be the soul of a dramatic performance, or entirely to be banished from it: if love is not tragical, it is insipid; and when it is tragical, it should reign alone; it was never made for a second place. It was Rotrou, or rather we must own, the great Corneille himself, who, in his creation of the stage, at the same time disfigured and disgraced it, by those ridiculous intrigues, bespoken, as it were, and made on purpose, those affairs of gallantry, which not being true passions, were unworthy of the stage; if you would know the reason why Corneille's tragedies are so seldom played, the reason is plain enough: it is because, in his "Otho."

"Otho makes a compliment to his mistress more like a man of wit than a real lover: he follows step by step the effort of his memory, which it is much more easy to admire than to believe. Camille herself seemed to be of his opinion; she would have liked much better a discourse less studied.—Tell me then, when Otho made love to Camille, was he contented, or was she kind?"

It is because in, "Pompey," Cleopatra—a useless character—says that Cæsar "sighs for her," and in a plaintive style calls himself "her captive, even in the field of victory."

It is because Cæsar asks Antony if he has seen this "adorable queen": to which Antony replies, "Yes, my lord, I have seen her, she is incomparable."

It is because, in "Sertorius," old Sertorius falls in love, not only because he likes the lady, but with a political view, and cries out: "I love: but it suits my age so ill to be in love, that I even conceal it from the fair one who has charmed me, as I know that the deep and yellow wrinkles on my forehead can have no great power in captivating the senses."

It is because, in "Œdipus," Theseus begins by saying to Dirce, "Whatever dreadful havoc the plague may make here, absence to true lovers is far more dreadful."

In a word, it is because such love as this will never make us shed tears; and when that passion does not affect us, it must be quite insipid.

I have said no more here, sir, than what all good judges, and men of taste, say to one another every day; what you have often heard at my house; in short, what everybody thinks, but none dare to publish: you know well enough the nature of mankind: half the world write in opposition to their own opinions, for fear of shocking received prejudices and vulgar errors. With regard to myself, who have never mixed any political reserve with my sentiments on literature, I speak the truth boldly, and will add, that I respect Corneille more, and have a higher opinion of the real merit of this great father of the stage, than those who praise him indiscriminately, and are blind to all his faults.

A "Mérope" was exhibited at London in 1731: who would have thought a love-intrigue could ever have been thought of at that time? But ever since the reign of Charles II. love has taken possession of the English stage; though there is not a nation upon earth by whom that passion is so ill painted; but the intrigue so absurdly brought in, and so badly treated, is the least fault of the English "Mérope." The young Ægisthus, delivered out of prison by a maid of honor, who is in love with him, is brought before the queen, who presents him with a bowl of poison, and a dagger, and speaks thus to him: "If you don't swallow the poison, this dagger shall put an end to your mistress' life." The young man drinks the poison, and is carried off in the agonies of death: he comes back in the fifth act coldly to inform Mérope that he is her son, and that he has slain the tyrant. Mérope asks him how this miracle was performed: to which he replies, that a friend of the maid of honor had put poppy-water, instead of poison, into the cup. "I was only asleep," says he, "when they thought me dead; I learned, when I awaked, that I was your son, and immediately killed the tyrant." Thus ends the tragedy; no doubt but it met with a bad reception: but is it not strange that it should ever have been represented? Is it not a proof that the English stage is not yet refined? It seems as if the same cause that deprives the English of any excellency in, or genius for, music and painting, takes from them also all perfection in tragedy. This island, which has produced the finest philosophers in the world, is not equally productive of the fine arts; and if the English do not seriously apply themselves to the study of those precepts which were given them by their excellent countrymen, Addison and Pope, they will never come near to other nations in point of taste and literature.

But whilst the subject of "Mérope" has been thus disgraced and disfigured in one part of Europe, it has met with better fate in Italy, where it has for a long time been treated in the true taste of the ancients. In this sixteenth century, which will be famous throughout all ages, the Count de Torelli gave us his "Mérope" with choruses. If in La Chapelle's tragedy we find all the faults of the French stage, such as useless intrigues, episodes, and a romantic air; and in the English author the highest degree of indecency, barbarism, and absurdity; we likewise meet in the Italian with all the faults of the Greek theatre, such as the want of action, and declamation. You, sir, have avoided all the rocks which they split upon; you, who have done honor to your country, by complete models of more than one kind, you have given us in your "Mérope" an example of a tragedy that is at once both simple and interesting.

The moment I read it I was struck with it; my love to my own country has never shut my eyes against the merit of foreigners. On the other hand, the more regard I have for it, the more I endeavor to enrich it, by the addition of treasures that are not of its own growth. The desire which I had of translating your "Mérope," was increased by the honor of a personal acquaintance with you at Paris, in the year 1733. By loving the author, I became still more enamored with his work; but when I sat down to it, I found it was impossible to bring it on the

French stage. We are grown excessively delicate: like the Sybarites of old, we are so immersed in luxury, that we cannot bear that rustic simplicity, and that description of a country life, which you have imitated from the Greek theatre. I am afraid our audiences would not suffer young Ægisthus to make a present of his ring to the man that stops him. I could not have ventured to seize upon a hero, and take him for a robber; though, at the same time, the circumstances he is in authorize the mistake. Our manners, which probably admit of many things which yours do not, would not permit us to represent the tyrant, the murderer of Mérope's husband and children, pretending, after fifteen years, to be in love with her; nor could I even have dared to make the queen say to him, "Why did not you talk to me of love before, when the bloom of youth was yet on my face?" Conversations of this kind are natural; but our pit, which at some times is so indulgent, and at others so nice and delicate, would think them perhaps too familiar, and might even discover coquetry, where, in reality, there might be nothing but what was just and proper. Our stage would by no means have suffered Mérope to bind her son to a pillar, nor to run after him with a javelin, and an axe in her hand, nor have permitted the young man to run away from her twice, and beg his life of the tyrant: much less could we have suffered the confidante of Mérope to have persuaded Ægisthus to go to sleep on the stage, merely to give the queen an opportunity of coming there to assassinate him: not but all this is natural: but you must pardon us for expecting that nature should always be presented to us with some strokes of art; strokes that are extremely different at Paris from those which we meet with at Verona.

To give you a proper idea of the different taste and judgment of polite and cultivated nations, with regard to the same arts, permit me here to quote a few passages from your own celebrated performance, which seem dictated by pure nature. The person who stops young Cresphontes, and takes the ring from him, says:

Or dunque in tuo paese i servi
Han di coteste gemme? un bel pacse
Sia questo tuo, nel nostro una tal gemma
Ad un dito real non sconverebbe.

I will take the liberty to translate this into blank verse, in which your tragedy is written, as I have not time at present to work it into rhyme.

Have slaves such precious jewels where thou livest?
Sure 'tis a noble country; for, with us,

Such rings might well adorn a royal hand.

The tyrant's confidant tells him, when speaking of the queen, who refuses, after twenty years, to marry the known murderer of her family:

La donna, come sai, ricusa e brama
Women, we know, refuse when most they love.

The queen's waiting-woman answers the tyrant, who presses her to use her influence in his favor, thus:

—dissimulato in vano
Soffre di febre assalto; alquanti giorni
Donare e forza a rinfrancar suoi spiriti.

The queen, sir has a fever, 'tis in vain
To hide it, and her spirits are oppressed;
She must have time to recollect them

In your fourth act, old Polydore asks one of Mérope's courtiers who he is? To which he replies, "I am Eurises, the son of Nicander." Polydore then, speaking of Nicander, talks in the style of Homer's Nestor.

—Egli cra humano
Eliberal, quando appariva, tutti
Faceangli honor; io mi ricordo ancora
Diquanto ei festeggio con bella pompa
Le sue nozze con Silvia, ch'era figlia
D'Olimpia e di Glicon fratel d'Ipparcho.
Ju dunque sir quel fanciullin che in corte
Silvia condur solea quasi per pompa;
Parmi' l'altir hieri: O quanto siete presti,
Quanto voi v'affrettate, O giovinetti,
A farvi adulti ed a gridar tacendo
Che noi diam loco!

The most humane, most generous of mankind,
Where'er he went, respected and beloved:
O I remember well the feast he gave

When to his Sylvia wedded, the fair daughter
Of Glycon, brother of the brave Hipparchus,
And chaste Olympia: and art thou that infant
Whom Sylvia to the court so often brought
And fondled in her arms? alas! methinks
It was but yesterday: how quickly youth
Shoots up, and tells us we must quit the scene!

In another place the same old man, being invited to the ceremony of the queen's marriage, says:

—Oh curioso
Punto io non son, passo stagione. Assai
Veduti ho sacrificii; io mi recordo
Di quello ancora quando il re Cresphonte
Incomincio a regnar. Quella fu pompa.
Ora piu non si fanno a questi tempi
Di cotai sacrificii. Piu di cento
Fur le beste sivenate i sacerdoti
Risplendean tutti, ed ove ti volgessi
Altro non si vedea che argento ed oro.

My time is past, and curiosity
Is now no more: already I have seen
Enough of nuptial rites, enough of pomp
And sacrifice: I still remember well
The great solemnity, when King Cresphontes
Began his reign: O 'twas a noble sight!
We cannot boast of such in these our days:
A hundred beasts were offered up, the priests
In all their splendor shone, and naught was seen
But gold and silver.—

All these strokes are natural, all agreeable to the characters and manners represented: such familiar dialogues would, no doubt, have been well received at Athens; but Paris and our pit expect a simplicity of another kind. We may, perhaps, even boast of a more refined taste than Athens itself, where, though the principal city of all Greece, it does not appear to me that they ever represented any theatrical pieces except on the four solemn festivals; whereas at

Paris there is always more than one every day in the year. At Athens the number of citizens was computed at only ten thousand, and Paris has nearly eight hundred thousand inhabitants; among whom, I suppose, we may reckon thirty thousand judges of dramatic performances, who really do pass their judgments almost every day of their lives.

In your tragedy you took the liberty to translate that elegant and simple comparison from Virgil.

Qualis populea maerens Philomela sub umbra
Amissos queritur faetus.

But if I were to take the same in mine, they would say it was fitter for an epic poem: such a rigid master have we to please in what we call the public:

Nescis, heu! nescis nostra fastidia Romae:
Et pueri nasum Rhinocerontis habent.

The English have a custom of finishing almost all their acts with a simile; but we expect that, in a tragedy, the hero should talk, and not the poet. Our audience is of opinion that in an important crisis of affairs, in a council, in a violent passion, or a pressing danger, princes and ministers should never make poetical comparisons.

How could I ever venture to make the under characters talk together for a long time? With you those conversations serve to prepare interesting scenes between the principal actors: they are like the avenues to a fine palace: but our spectators are for coming into it at once. We must therefore comply with the national taste, which is, perhaps, grown more difficult, from having been cloyed, as it were, with such a variety of fine performances: and yet among these recitals, which our excessive severity condemns, how many beauties do I regret the loss of! How does simple nature delight me, though beneath a form that appears strange to us!

I have here, sir, given you some of those reasons which prevailed on me not to follow what I so much admired. I was obliged, not without regret, to write a new "Mérope"; I have done it in a different manner, but I am far from thinking that I have therefore done it better. I look upon myself, with regard to you, as a traveller to whom an eastern monarch had made a present of some very rich stuffs: the king would certainly permit this traveller to wear them according to the fashion of his own country.

My "Mérope" was finished in the beginning of the year 1736, pretty nearly as it now stands; studies of another kind prevented me from bringing it on the stage: but what weighed most with me was, the hazard which I ran in producing it, after several successful pieces on almost the same subject, though under different names. At length, however, I ventured to produce it, and the public gave me a convincing proof that they could condescend to see the same matter worked up in a different manner. That happened to our stage which we see every day in a gallery of pictures, where there are many of them on exactly the same subject. The judges are pleased by the observation of these different manners, and everyone marks down and enjoys, according to his own taste, the character of every painter. This is a kind of happy concurrence, which, at the same time that it contributes towards the perfection of the Art, gives the public a better insight into it. If the French "Mérope" has met with the same success as the Italian, it is to you, sir, I am indebted for it; to that simplicity in your performance which I have taken for my model, and which I was always an admirer of. Though I walked in a different path, you were always my guide. I could have wished, after the examples of the Italians and English, to employ the happy facility of blank verse, and have often called to mind this passage of "Rucellai":

Tu sai purche l' imagine della voce
Che risponde da i sassi, dove l' echo alberga.
Sempre nemica fu del nostro regno,
E fu inventrice delle prime rime.

But I am satisfied, as I have long since declared, that such an attempt would never succeed in France, and it would be rather a mark of weakness than good sense, to endeavor to shake off a yoke which so many authors have borne, whose works will last as long as the nation itself. Our poetry has none of those liberties which yours has; and this is perhaps one of the reasons why the Italians got the start of us, by three or four centuries, in this most difficult and most delightful art.

As I have endeavored to imitate you in tragedy, I should be glad to follow your example in other branches of literature, for which you are so eminently distinguished: I could wish to form my taste by yours in the science of history; I do not mean the empty, barren knowledge of dates and facts, that only informs us at what period of time a man died, who perhaps was a useless or a pernicious member of society; the science of lexicography, that loads the memory without improving the mind; I mean that history of the human heart which teaches us men and manners, which leads us from error to error, and from prejudice to prejudice, into the effects of the various passions and affections that agitate mankind: which shows us all the evils that ignorance, or knowledge misapplied, has produced in the world; and which, above all, gives us a clue to the progress of the arts, and follows them through the dangers of so many contending powers, and the ruin of so many empires.

It is this which makes history delightful; and it becomes still more so to me, by the place which you will possess amongst those who have pleased and instructed mankind. It will raise the emulation of posterity, to hear that your country has bestowed on you the most signal honors, that Verona has raised a statue, with this inscription, "To the Marquis Scipio Maffei in his lifetime"—an inscription as beautiful in its kind as that at Montpellier to Louis XIV. after his death.

Deign, sir, to accept, with the respects of your fellow-citizens, those of a stranger, who esteems and honors you as much as if he had been born at Verona.

A Letter from M. de la Lindelle to M. de Voltaire.

Sir:
You had the politeness to dedicate your tragedy of "Mérope" to M. Maffei, and have served the cause of literature both in Italy and France, by pointing out, from the perfect knowledge which you have of the theatre, the different rules and conduct of the Italian and French stages. The partial attachment which you have to everything that comes from Italy, added to your particular regard for M. Maffei, would not permit you to censure the real faults of that excellent writer; but as I have myself nothing in view but truth, and the advancement of the arts, I shall not be afraid to speak the sentiments of the judicious public, and which I am satisfied must be yours also.

The Abbé Desfontaines had already remarked some palpable errors in the "Mérope" of M. Maffei; but, according to his usual manner, with more rudeness than justice, he has mingled a few good criticisms with many bad ones. This satirist, so universally decried, had neither knowledge enough of the Italian tongue, nor taste enough to form an equitable judgment.

This, then, is the opinion of the most judicious amongst those literati whom I have consulted, both in France and on the other side of the Alps. "Mérope" appears to every one of them, past dispute, the most interesting and truly tragic subject that was ever brought on the stage, infinitely beyond that of "Athalie"; because Athalie does not want to assassinate the young king, but is deceived by the High-Priest, who seeks revenge on her for her former crimes: whereas in Mérope we see a mother, who, in avenging her son, is on the point of murdering that very son himself, her only desire, and her only hope: the interest of "Mérope" therefore affects us in a very different manner from that of "Athalie": but it seems as if M. Maffei was satisfied with what the subject naturally suggested to him, without making use of any theatrical art in the conduct of it.

1. The scenes in many places are not linked together, and the stage is left void; a fault which, in the present age, is looked upon as unpardonable, even in the lowest class of dramatic writers.

2. The actors frequently come in and go out without reason; a fault no less considerable.

3. There is no probability, no dignity, no decorum, no art in the dialogue: in the very first scene we see a tyrant reasoning in the calmest manner with Mérope, whose husband and children he had murdered, and making love to her: this would have been hissed at Paris, even by the poorest judges.

4. While the tyrant is thus ridiculously making love to the old queen, word is brought that they have found a young man who had committed murder; but it does not appear through the whole course of the play who it was he had killed: he pretends it was a thief, who wanted to steal his clothes. How low, little and poor is this! It would not be borne in a farce at a country fair.

5. The captain of the guard, provost, or whatever you call him, examines the murderer, who has a fine ring upon his finger: this scene is quite low comedy, and the style is agreeable to it, and worthy of the scene.

6. The mother immediately supposes that the robber, who was killed, is her son. It is pardonable, no doubt, in a mother to fear everything; but a queen who is a mother should have required better proofs.

7. In the midst of all these fears, the tyrant Poliphontes reasons with Mérope's waiting-woman about his pretended passion. These cold and indecent scenes, which are only brought in to fill up the act, would never be suffered on a regular stage. You have only, sir, modestly taken notice of one of these scenes, where Mérope's woman desires the tyrant not to hasten the nuptials; because, she says, her mistress has "an attack of a fever": but I, sir, will boldly aver, in the name of all the critics, that such a conversation, and such an answer, are only fit for Harlequin's theatre.

8. I will add, moreover, that when the queen, imagining her son to be dead, tells us she longs to pull the heart out of the murderer's breast, and tear it with her teeth, she talks more like a cannibal than an afflicted mother; and that decency should be preserved in everything.

9. Ægisthus, who was brought in as a robber, and who had said that he had himself been attacked, is taken for a thief a second time, and carried before the queen, in spite of the king, who notwithstanding undertakes to defend him. The queen binds him to a pillar, is going to kill him with a dart; but before she throws it, asks him some questions. Ægisthus tells her, that his father is an old man, upon which the queen immediately relents. Is not this an excellent reason for changing her mind, and imagining that Ægisthus might be her own son? a most indisputable mark to be sure: is it so very extraordinary that a young man should have an old father? Maffei has added this absurdity, this deficiency of art and genius, to another even more ridiculous, which he had made in his first edition. Ægisthus says to the queen, "O Polydore, my father." This Polydore was the very man to whom Mérope had entrusted the care of Ægisthus. At hearing the name of Polydore, the queen could no longer doubt that Ægisthus was her son: thus the piece was entirely at an end. This error was removed; but removed, we see, only to make room for a greater.

10. While the queen is thus ridiculously, and without any reason, in suspense, occasioned by the mention of an old man, the tyrant comes in, and takes Ægisthus under his protection. The young man, who should have been represented as a hero, thanks the king for his life, with a base and mean submission that is disgusting, and entirely degrades the character of Ægisthus.

11. At length Mérope and the tyrant are left together: Mérope exhausts her resentment in reproaches without end. Nothing can be more cold and lifeless than these scenes, full of declamation, that have no plot, interest, or contrasted passion in them; they are schoolboy scenes: everything in a play, that is without action, is useless.

12. There is so little art in this piece that the author is always forced to employ confidants to fill up the stage. The fourth act begins with another cold and useless scene between the tyrant and the queen's waiting-woman, who, a little afterwards, lights, we know not how, on young Ægisthus, and persuades him to rest himself in the porch, merely to give the queen a fair opportunity of despatching him when he falls asleep; which he does according to promise. An excellent plot this! and then the queen comes a second time, with an axe in her hand, in order to kill the young man, who is gone to sleep for that purpose. This circumstance, twice repeated, is surely the height of barrenness, as the young man's sleep is the height of ridicule. M. Maffei thinks there is genius and variety in this repetition, because the queen comes in the first time with a dart, and the second with an axe. What a strange effect of fancy!

13. At last old Polydore comes in apropos, and prevents the queen from striking the blow. One would naturally imagine that this happy instant must

produce a thousand affecting incidents between the mother and son; but we meet with nothing of this kind: Ægisthus flies off, and sees no more of his mother: he has not so much as one scene with her. This betrays a want of genius that is insupportable. Mérope asks the old man what recompense he demands; and the old fool begs her to make him young again. In this manner the queen employs her time, which doubtless she should have spent in running after her son: all this is low, ill-placed, and ridiculous to the last degree.

14. In the course of this piece the tyrant is always for espousing Mérope; and, to compass his end, he bids her agents tell her, that he will murder all her servants, if she does not consent to give him her hand. What a ridiculous idea, and how extravagant a tyrant! Could not M. Maffei have found out a more specious pretext to save the honor of a queen, who had meanness enough to marry the murderer of her whole family?

15. Another childish college trick: the tyrant says to his confidant, "I know the art of reigning; I'll put the bold and rebellious to death; give the reins to all kinds of vice; invite my subjects to commit the most atrocious crimes, and pardon the most guilty; expose the good to the fury of the wicked." Did ever man pronounce such vile stuff? This declamation of a regent of sixteen, does it not give us a fine idea of a man who knows how to govern? Racine was condemned for having made Mathan—in his "Athalie"—say too much against himself; and yet Mathan talks reasonably: but here it is to the last degree absurd to pretend, that throwing everything into confusion is the art of ruling well; it is rather the art of dethroning himself. One cannot read anything so ridiculous without laughing at it. M. Maffei is a strange politician.

In a word, sir, this work of Maffei is a fine subject, but a very bad performance. Everybody at Paris agrees that it would not go through one representation; and the sensible men in Italy have a very poor opinion of it. It is in vain the author has taken so much pains in his travels, to engage the worst writers he could pick up to translate his tragedy: it was much easier for him to pay a translator, than to make his piece a good one.

The Answer of M. de Voltaire to M. de la Lindelle.

Sir:

The letter which you did me the honor to write to me entitles you to the name of "Hypercritic," which was given to the famous Scaliger; you are truly a most redoubtable adversary; if you treat M. Maffei in this manner, what am I to expect from you? I acknowledge that, in many points, you have too much reason on your side. You have taken a great deal of pains to rake together a heap of brambles and briars; but why would you not enjoy the pleasure of gathering a few flowers? There are certainly many in M. Maffei; and which, I dare affirm, will flourish forever. Such are the scenes between the mother and son, and the narration of the catastrophe. I can't help thinking that these strokes are affecting and pathetic. You say, the subject alone makes all the beauty; but was it not the same subject in other authors who have treated Mérope? Why, with the same assistance, had they not the same success? Does not this single argument prove, that M. Maffei owes as much to his genius as to his subject?

To be plain with you, I think M. Maffei has shown more art than myself, in the manner by which he has contrived to make Mérope think that her son is the murderer of her son. I could not bring myself to make use of the ring as he did; because, after the royal ring that Boilieu laughs at in his satires, this circumstance would always appear too trifling on our stage. We must conform to the fashions of our own age and nation; and, for the same reason, we ought not lightly to condemn those of foreigners.

Neither M. Maffei nor I have sufficiently explained the motives that should so strongly incline Poliphontes to espouse the queen. This is, perhaps, a fault inherent in the subject; but I must own I think this fault very inconsiderable, when the circumstances it produces are so interesting. The grand point is to affect and draw tears from the spectators. Tears were shed both at Verona and at Paris. This is the best answer that can be made to the critics. It is impossible to be perfect; but how meritorious is it to move an audience, in spite of all our imperfections! Most certain it is, that in Italy many things are passed over, which would not be pardoned in France: first, because taste, decorum, and the stage itself, are not the same in both; secondly, because the Italians, having no city where they represent dramatic pieces every day, cannot possibly be so used to things of this kind as ourselves. Opera, that splendid monster, has driven Melpomene from among them; and there are so many of the Castrati there, that no room is left for Roscius and Æsopus: but if ever the Italians should have a regular theatre, I believe they would soon get beyond us: their stages are more extensive, their language more tractable, their blank verses easier to be made, their nation possessed of more sensibility; but they want encouragement, peace, and plenty.

ACT I.

SCENE I.

Scene at Messene, in the Palace of Mérope.

Ismenia, Mérope.

Ismenia: Let not, great queen, thy soul forever dwell On images of horror and despair; The storm is past, and brighter days succeed: Long hast thou tasted heaven's severest wrath, Enjoy its bounties now: the gods, thou seest, Have blessed our land with victory and peace; And proud Messene, after fifteen years Of foul division and intestine wars, Now from her ruins lifts her towering front, Superior to misfortune: now no more Shalt thou behold her angry chiefs support Their jarring interests, and in guilt alone United, spread destruction, blood and slaughter, O'er half thy kingdom, and dispute the throne Of good Cresphontes: but the ministers Of heaven, the guardians of our sacred laws, The rulers, and the people, soon shall meet, Free in their choice, to fix the power supreme: If virtue gives the diadem, 'tis thine: Thine by irrevocable right: to thee, The widow of Cresphontes, from our kings Descended, must devolve Messene's throne: Thou, whom misfortunes and firm constancy Have made but more illustrious, and more dear; Thou, to whom every heart in secret tied—

Mérope: No news of Narbas! shall I never see My child again?

Ismenia: Despair not, madam: slaves Have been despatched on every side; the paths Of Elis all are open to their search: Doubtless the object of your fears is placed In faithful hands, who will restore to you Their sacred trust.

Mérope: Immortal gods! who see My bitter griefs, will ye restore my son? Is my Ægisthus living? have you saved My wretched infant? O preserve him still, And shield him from the cruel murderer's hand! He is your son, the pure, the spotless blood Of your Alcides. Will you not protect The dear, dear image of the best of men, The best of kings, whose ashes I adore?

Ismenia: But wherefore must this tender passion turn Thy soul aside from every other purpose?

Mérope: I am a mother: canst thou wonder yet?

Ismenia: A mother's fondness should not thus efface The duty of a queen, your character, And noble rank; though in his infant years You loved this son, yet little have you seen Or known of him.

Mérope: Not seen him, my Ismenia? O he is always present to my heart, Time has no power to loose such bonds as these; His danger still awakens all my fears, And doubles my affection: once I've heard From Narbas, and but once these four years past, And that alas! but made me more unhappy. "Ægisthus," then he told me, "well deserves A better fate; he's worthy of his mother. And of the gods, his great progenitors: Exposed to every ill, his virtue braves, And will surmount them: hope for everything From him, but be aware of Poliphontes."

Ismenia: Prevent him then, and take the reins of empire In your own hands.

Mérope: That empire is my son's: Perdition on the cruel step-mother, The lover of herself, the savage heart, That could enjoy the pleasures of a throne, And disinherit her own blood! O no: Ismenia, If my Ægisthus lives not, what is empire. Or what is life to me! I should renounce them. I should have died when my unhappy lord Was basely slain, by men and gods betrayed. O perfidy! O guilt! O fatal day! O death! forever present to my sight! Methinks even now I hear the dismal shrieks, I hear them cry, "O save the king, his wife, His sons;" I see the walls all stained with blood, The flaming palace, helpless women crushed Beneath the smoking ruins, fear and tumult On every side, arms, torches, death, and horror: Then, rolled in dust, and bathing in his blood, Cresphontes pressed me to his arms, upraised His dying eyes, and took his last farewell; Whilst his two hapless babes, the tender fruits Of our first love, thrown on the bleeding bosom Of their dead father, lifted up the hands Of innocence, and begged me to protect them Against the barbarous murderers: Ægisthus Alone escaped: some god defended him. O thou who didst protect his infancy Watch o'er and guard him, bring him to my eyes; O let him from inglorious solitude Rise to the rank of his great ancestors! I've borne his absence long, and groaned in chains These fifteen years: now let Ægisthus reign Instead of Mérope: for all my pains And sorrows past, be that the great reward.

SCENE II.

Mérope, Ismenia, Euricles.

Mérope: Well! what of Narbas, and my son?

Euricles: [Confused] I stand before thee; all our cares are vain; We've searched the banks of Peneus, and the fields Of fair Olympia, even to the walls Of proud Salmoneus, but no Narbas there Is to be found or heard of, not a trace Remaining of him.

Mérope: Narbas is no more, And all is lost.

Ismenia: Whatever thy fears suggest Thou still believest; and yet who knows but now, Even whilst we speak, the happy Narbas comes To crown thy wishes, and restore thy son.

Euricles: Perhaps his love, tempered with fair discretion, Which long concealed Ægisthus from the eyes Of men, may hide his purposed journey from thee: He dreads the murderer's hand, and still protects him From those who slew Cresphontes: we must strive By artful methods to elude the rage That cannot be opposed: I have secured Their passage hither, and have placed some friends Of most approved valor, whose sharp eyes Will look abroad, and safe conduct them to thee.

Mérope: I've placed my surest confidence in thee.

Euricles: But what alas! can all my watchfulness And faithful cares avail thee, when the people Already meet to rob thee of thy right, And place another on Messene's throne? Injustice triumphs, and the shameless crowd, In proud contempt of sacred laws, incline To Poliphontes.

Mérope: Am I fallen so low: And shall my son return to be a slave? To see a subject raised to the high rank Of his great ancestors, the blood of Jove Debased, degraded, forced to own a master. Have I no friend, no kind protector left? Ungrateful subjects! have you no regard, No reverence for the memory of Cresphontes? Have you so soon forgot his glorious deeds, His goodness to you?

Euricles: Still his name is dear, Still they regret him, still they weep his fate, And pity thine: but power intimidates, And makes them dread the wrath of Poliphontes.

Mérope: Thus, by my people still oppressed, I see Justice give way to faction, interest still, The arbiter of fate, sells needy virtue To powerful guilt; the weak must to the strong Forever yield: but let us hence, and strive To fire once more their coward hearts to rage And fierce resentment, for the injured blood Of Hercules: excite the people's love; Flatter their hopes; O tell them, Euricles, Their master is returned.

Euricles: I've said too much Already; Poliphontes is alarmed: He dreads your son; he dreads your very tears: Restless ambition, that holds nothing dear Or sacred but itself, has filled his soul With bitterness and pride: because he drove The ruffian slaves from Pylos and Amphrysa, And saved Messene from a band of robbers, He claims it as his conquest: for himself Alone he acts, and would enslave us all: He looks towards the crown, and to attain it Would throw down every fence, break every law, Spill any blood that shall oppose him: they Who killed thy husband were not more revengeful, More bloody, than the cruel Poliphontes.

Mérope: I am entangled in some fatal snare On every side, danger and guilt surround me: This Poliphontes, this ambitious subject, Whose crimes—

Euricles: He's here: you must dissemble.

SCENE III.

Mérope, Poliphontes, Erox.

Euricles: Madam, At length I come to lay my heart before you: I've served the state, and my successful toils Have opened me a passage to the throne: The assembled chiefs awhile suspend their choice, But soon must fix it, or on Mérope, Or Poliphontes: the unhappy feuds That laid Messene waste, and filled the land With blood and slaughter, all are buried now In peaceful harmony, and we alone Remain to part the fair inheritance. We should support each other's mutual claim; Our common interest, and our common foes, Love for our country, reason, duty, all Conspire to join us, all unite to say The warrior who avenged thy husband, he Who saved thy kingdom, may aspire to thee. I know these hoary locks, and wrinkled brow, Have little charms to please a youthful fair one. Thou'rt in the bloom of spring, and mayest despise The winter of my days; but statesmen heed not Such fond objections: let the royal wreath Hide these gray hairs, a sceptre and a queen Will recompense my toils: nor think me rash, Or vain, you are the daughter of a king, I know you are, but your Messene wants A master now; therefore remember, madam, If you would keep your right, you must—divide it.

Mérope: Heaven, that afflicts me with its bitterest woes, Prepared me not for this, this cruel insult: How darest thou ask it? wert thou not the subject Of great Cresphontes? thinkest thou I will e'er Betray the memory of my dearest lord, To share with thee his son's inheritance, Trust to thy hands his kingdom and his mother? Thinkest thou the royal wreath was made to bind A soldier's brows?

Euricles: That soldier has a right To rule the kingdom which his arm defended. What was the first that bore the name of king, But a successful soldier? he who serves His country well requires not ancestry To make him noble: the inglorious blood, Which I received from him who gave me life, I shed already in my country's cause, It flowed for thee; and, spite of thy proud scorn, I must at least be equal to the kings I have subdued: but, to be brief with you, The throne will soon be mine, and Mérope May share it with me, if her pride will deign To accept it: I've a powerful party, madam.

Mérope: A party! wretch, to trample on our laws: Is there a party which thou darest support Against the king's, against the royal race? Is this thy faith, thy solemn vows, thy oath, Sworn to Cresphontes, and to me; the love, The honor due to his illustrious shade, His wretched widow, and his hapless son; The gods he sprang from, and the throne they gave?

Euricles: 'Tis doubtful whether yet your son survives; But grant that, from the mansions of the dead, He should return, and in the face of heaven Demand his throne, believe me when I say He would demand in vain; Messene wants A master worthy of her, one well proved, A king who could defend her: he alone Should wield the sceptre who can best avenge His country's cause: Ægisthus is a child, Yet unexperienced in the ways of men, And therefore little will his birth avail him; Naught hath he done for us, and naught deserved: He cannot purchase at so cheap a rate Messene's throne, the right of power supreme

Defends no more the gift of nature, here From son to son; it is the price of toil, Of labor, and of blood; 'tis virtue's meed, Which I shall claim: have you so soon forgot The savage sons of Pylos and Amphrysa, Those lawless plunderers? Think on your Cresphontes, And your defenceless children whom they slew: Who saved your country then? Who stopped their fury? Who put your foes to flight, and chased them hence? Did not this arm avenge that murdered lord Whom yet you weep? these, madam, are my rights, The rights of valor: this is all my rank, This all my title, and let heaven decide it. If thy Ægisthus comes, by me perhaps He may be taught to live, by me to reign: Then shall he see how Poliphontes guides The reins of empire. I esteem the blood Of great Alcides, but I fear it not; I look beyond Alcides' race, and fain Would imitate the god from whom he sprung: I would defend the mother, serve the son; Be an example to him, and a father.

Mérope: O, sir, no more of your affected cares; Your generous offers, meant but to insult My hapless son; if you would wish to tread In great Alcides' steps, reserve the crown For his descendant: know, that demi-god Was the avenger of wronged innocence; No ravisher, no tyrant; take thou care, And with his valor imitate his justice; Protect the guiltless, and defend your king, Else shalt thou prove a worthless successor. If thou wouldst gain the mother, seek the son; Go, bring him to me; bring your master here, And then perhaps I may descend to you: But I will never be the vile accomplice, Or the reward, of guilt like thine.

SCENE IV.

Poliphontes, Erox.

Erox: My lord, Did you expect to move her? Does the throne Depend on her capricious will? Must she Conduct you to it?

Euricles: 'Twixt that throne and me, Erox, I see a dreadful precipice I must o'erleap, or perish: Mérope Expects Ægisthus; and the fickle crowd, If he returns, perhaps may bend towards him. In vain his father's and his brothers' blood, Have opened wide my passage to the throne; In vain hath fortune cast her friendly veil O'er all my crimes; in vain have I oppressed The blood of kings, whilst the deluded people Adored me as their friend, if yet there lives A hateful offspring of Alcides' race: If this lamented son should e'er again Behold Messene, fifteen years of toil At once are lost, and all my hopes o'erthrown; All the fond prejudice of birth and blood Will soon revive the memory of Cresphontes, A hundred kings for his proud ancestors, The boasted honor of a race divine, A mother's tears, her sorrows, her despair, All will conspire to shake my feeble power: Ægisthus is a foe I must subdue: I would have crushed the serpent in his shell, But that the diligent and subtle Narbas Conveyed him hence, e'er since that time concealed In some far distant land, he hath escaped My narrowest search, and baffled all my care: I stopped his couriers, broke the intelligence 'Twixt him and Mérope; but fortune oft Deserts us: from the silence of oblivion Sometimes a secret may spring forth; and heaven, By slow and solemn steps, may bring down vengeance.

Erox: Depend, undaunted, on thy prosperous fate; Prudence, thy guardian god, shall still protect thee: Thy orders are obeyed; the soldiers watch Each avenue of Elis and Messene: If Narbas brings Ægisthus here, they both Must die.

Euricles: But say, canst thou depend on those Whom thou hast placed to intercept them?

Erox: Yes: None of them know whose blood is to be shed, Or the king's name whom they must sacrifice. Narbas is painted to them as a traitor, A guilty vagabond, that seeks some place Of refuge; and the other, as a slave, A murderer, to be yielded up to justice.

Euricles: It must be so: this crime and I have done; And yet, when I have rid me of the son, I must possess the mother: 'twill be useful: I shall not then be branded with the name Of a usurper; she will bring with her A noble portion in the people's love: I know their hearts are not inclined to me; With fears dejected, or inflamed with hope, Still in extremes, the giddy multitude Tumultuous rove, and interest only binds them, That makes them mine. Erox, thy fate depends On my success; thou art my best support: Go, and unite them; bribe the sordid wretch With gold to serve me, let the subtle courtier Expect my favors; raise the coward soul, Inspire the valiant, and caress the bold; Persuade and promise, threaten and implore: Thus far this sword hath brought me on my way; But what by courage was begun, by art We must complete; that many-headed monster, The people, must be soothed by flattery's power: I'm feared already, but I would be loved.

ACT II.

SCENE I.

Mérope, Euricles, Ismenia.

Mérope: Hast thou heard nothing of my dear Ægisthus? No news from Elis' frontiers? O, too well I know the cause of this ill-boding silence!

Euricles: In all our search we have discovered naught, Save a young stranger, reeking with the blood Of one whom he had murdered: we have chained, And brought him hither.

Mérope: Ha! a murderer, A stranger too! Whom, thinkest thou, he has slain? My blood runs cold.

Euricles: The mere effect of love And tenderness: each little circumstance Alarms a soul like thine, that ever dwells On one sad object; 'tis the voice of nature, And will be heard; but let not this disturb thee, A common accident: our borders long Have been infested with these ruffian slaves, The baneful fruit of our intestine broils; Justice hath lost her power; our husbandmen Call on the gods for vengeance, and lament The blood of half their fellow-citizens, Slain by each other's hand: but, be composed, These terrors are not thine.

Mérope: Who is this stranger? Answer me, tell me.

Euricles: Some poor nameless wretch, Such he appears; brought up to infamy, To guilt, and sorrow.

Mérope: Well, no matter who, Or what he is; let him be brought before me. Important truths are often brought to light By meanest instruments. Perhaps my soul Is too much moved; pity a woman's weakness, Pity a mother, who has all to fear, And nothing to neglect: let him appear; I'll see, and question him.

Euricles: Your orders, madam, Shall be obeyed. [To Ismenia.] Tell them to bring him here, Before the queen.

Mérope: I know my cares are vain; But grief overpowers, and hurries me to act Perhaps imprudent; but you know I've cause For my despair; they have dethroned my son, And would insult the mother: Poliphontes Hath taken advantage of my helpless state, And dared to offer me his hand.

Euricles: Thy woes Are greater even than thou thinkest they are. I know this marriage would debase thy honor, And yet I see it must be so; thy fate Hath bound thee to it by the cruel tie Of dire necessity: I know it wears A dreadful aspect, yet perchance may prove The only means of placing on the throne Its rightful master, so the assembled chiefs And soldiers think; they with—

Mérope: My son would ne'er Consent to that: no: poverty and exile, With all their pains, were far less dreadful to him Than these base nuptials.

Euricles: If to assert his rights Alone sufficed to seat him on the throne, Doubtless his pride would spurn the shameful bond: But if his soul is by misfortune taught To know itself, if prudence guides his steps, If his own interest, if his friends' advice, And above all, necessity, the first Of human laws, have any influence o'er him, He would perceive, that his unhappy mother Could not bestow on him a dearer mark Of her affection.

Mérope: Ha! what sayest thou?

Euricles: Truth, Unwelcome truth, which nothing but my zeal, And your misfortunes, should have wrested from me.

Mérope: Wouldst thou persuade me then, that interest e'er Can get the better of my fixed aversion For Poliphontes, you who painted him In blackest colors to me?

Euricles: I described him Even as he is, most dangerous and bold; I know his rashness, and I know his power; Naught can resist him, he's without an heir. Remember that: you say, you love Ægisthus.

Mérope: I do; and 'tis that love which makes the tyrant Still more detested: wherefore talkest thou thus Of marriage and of empire? speak to me Of my dear son; and tell me if he lives; Inform me, Euricles.

Euricles: Behold the stranger Whom you desired to question; see, he comes.

SCENE II.

Mérope, Euricles, Ægisthus in Chains, Ismenia, Guards.

Ægisthus: [At the bottom of the stage. To Ismenia.] Is that the great unfortunate, the queen, Whose glory and whose sorrows reached even me Amidst the desert wild where I was hid?

Ismenia: 'Tis she.

Ægisthus: Thou great creator of mankind! Thou, who didst form those matchless charms, look down And guard thy image: virtue on a throne Is sure the first and fairest work of heaven.

Mérope: Is that the murderer? Can such features hide A cruel heart? Come near, unhappy youth, Be not alarmed, but answer me; whose blood Is on thy hands?

Ægisthus: O, queen, forgive me; fear, Respect, and grief, bind up my trembling lips. [Turning to Euricles.] I cannot speak; her presence shakes my soul With terror and amazement.

Mérope: Tell me whom Thy arm has slain.

Ægisthus: Some bold presumptuous youth, Whom fate condemned to fall the wretched victim Of his own rashness.

Mérope: Ha! a youth! my blood Runs cold within me: didst thou know him?

Ægisthus: No: Messene's walls, her fields, and citizens, Are new to me.

Mérope: And did this unknown youth Attack thee then? 'twas in thy own defence?

Ægisthus: Heaven is my witness, I am innocent. Just on the borders of Pamisus, where A temple stands, sacred to Hercules, Thy great progenitor, I offered up To the avenger of wronged innocence My humble prayers for thee; I had no victims, No precious gifts to lay before him; all I had to give him, was a spotless heart, And simple vows, the poor man's hecatomb: It seemed as if the god received my homage With kind affection, for I felt my heart By more than common resolution fired: Two men, both armed, and both unknown, surprised me; One in the bloom of youth, the other sunk Into the vale of years: "What brings thee here?" They cried, "and wherefore for Alcides' race Art thou a suppliant?" At this word they raised The dagger to my breast: but heaven preserved me. Pierced o'er with wounds, the youngest of them fell Dead at my feet; the other basely fled, Like an assassin: knowing not what blood I might have shed, and doubtful of my fate, I threw the bloody corpse into the sea, And fled; your soldiers stopped me; at the name Of Mérope, I yielded up my arms, And they have brought me hither.

Euricles: Why these tears, My royal mistress?

Mérope: Shall I own it to thee? I melted with compassion, as he told His melancholy tale; I know not why, But my heart sympathized with his distress: It cannot be, I blush to think it, yet Methought I traced the features of Cresphontes: Cruel remembrance! wherefore am I mocked With such deceitful images as these, Such fond delusions?

Euricles: Do not then embrace Such vain suspicions, he's not that barbarian, That vile impostor, which we thought him.

Mérope: No: Heaven hath imprinted on his open front The marks of candor, and of honesty. Where wert thou born?

Ægisthusin: In Elis.

Mérope: Ha! in Elis! In Elis! sayst thou? Knowst thou aught of Narbas, Or of Ægisthus? Never hath that name Yet reached thine ear? What rank, condition, friends, Who was thy father?

Ægisthusin: Polycletes, madam, A poor old man: to Narbas, or Ægisthus, Of whom thou speakest, I am a stranger.

Mérope: Gods! Why mock ye thus a poor unhappy mortal? A little dawn of hope just gleamed upon me, And now my eyes are plunged in deepest night: Say, what rank did thy parents hold in Greece?

Ægisthusin: If virtue made nobility, old Sirris And Polycletes, from whose blood I sprang, Are not to be despised: their lot indeed Was humble, but their exemplary virtues Made even poverty respectable: Clothed in his rustic garb, my honest father Obeys the laws, does all the good he can, And only fears the gods.

Mérope: [Aside.] How strangely he affects me! every word Has some new charm: [Turning to Ægisthus.] But wherefore left you then The good old man? It must be dreadful to him To lose a son like thee.

Ægisthusin: A fond desire Of glory led me hither: I had heard Of your Messene's troubles, and your own: Oft had I heard of the illustrious queen, Whose virtues merited a better fate; The sad recital moved my soul; ashamed To spend at Elis my inglorious days, I longed to brave the terrors of the field Beneath thy banners: this was my design, And this alone: an idle thirst of fame Misled my steps, and in their helpless age Persuaded me to leave my wretched parents: 'Tis my first fault, and I have suffered for it: Heaven hath avenged their cause, and I am fallen Into a fatal snare.

Mérope: 'Tis plain he is not, Cannot be guilty; falsehood never dwells With such ingenuous, sweet simplicity: Heaven has conducted here this hapless youth, And I will stretch the hand of mercy to him: It is enough for me he is a man, And most unfortunate; my son perhaps Even now laments his more distressful fate: O he recalls Ægisthus to my thoughts: Their age the same; perhaps Ægisthus now Wanders like him from clime to clime, unknown, Unpitied, suffers all the bitter woes And cruel scorn that waits on penury: Misery like this will bend the firmest soul, And wither all its virtues: lot severe For a king's offspring, and the blood of gods! O if at least—

SCENE III.

Mérope, Ægisthus, Euricles, Ismenia.

Ismenia: Hark! madam, heard you not Their loud tumultuous cries? You know not what—

Mérope: Whence are thy fears?

Ismenia: 'Tis Poliphontes' triumph: The wavering people flatter his ambition, And give their voices for him; he is chosen Messene's king: 'tis done.

Ægisthusin: I thought the gods Had on the throne of her great ancestors Placed Mérope: O heaven! the greater still Our rank on earth, the more have we to fear: A poor abandoned exile, like myself, Is less to be lamented than a queen: But we have all our sorrows. [Ægisthus is led off.]

Euricles: [To Mérope.] I foretold it: You were to blame to scorn his proffered hand, And brave his power.

Mérope: I see the precipice That opens wide its horrid gulf before me; But men and gods deceived me; I expected Justice from both, and both refused to grant it.

Euricles: I will assemble yet our little force Of trusty friends, to anchor our poor bark, And save it from the fury of the storm; To shield thee from the insults of a tyrant, And the mad rage of an ungrateful people.

SCENE IV.

Mérope, Ismenia.

Ismenia: 'Tis not the people's fault; they love you still, And would preserve the honor of your crown: They wish to see you joined to Poliphontes, That from your hand he then might seem to hold The sovereign power.

Mérope: They give me to a tyrant, Betray Ægisthus, and enslave his mother.

Ismenia: They call you to the throne of your forefathers: Obey their voice; it is the voice of heaven.

Mérope: And wouldst thou have me purchase empty honors With infamy and shame?

SCENE V.

Mérope, Euricles, Ismenia.

Euricles: O queen, I tremble To stand before thee: now prepare thy heart For the most dreadful stroke; call forth thy courage To bear the news.

Mérope: I have no courage left, 'Tis worn out by misfortune; but no matter. Proceed, inform me.

Euricles: All is past; and fate— I can no more.

Mérope: Go on: my son—

Euricles: He's dead: It is too true: the dreadful news hath shocked Your friends, and froze their active zeal.

Mérope: My son, Ægisthus, dead!

Ismenia: O gods!

Euricles: Some base assassins Had in his passage laid the snares of death; The horrid crime is done.

Mérope: O hateful day! Why shines the sun on such a wretch as I? He's lost; he's gone: what cruel hand destroyed him! Who shed his blood, the last of my sad race?

Euricles: It was that stranger, that abandoned slave, Whose persecuted virtue you admired, For whom such pity rose in your kind breast; Even he whom you protected.

Mérope: Can it be! Was he that monster?

Euricles: We have certain proofs, And have discovered two of his companions, Who, lurking here, were still in search of Narbas, Who had escaped them: he who slew Ægisthus Had taken from your son these precious spoils, [The armor is shown at a distance at the farther end of the stage.] The armor which old Narbas bore from hence. The traitor, that he might not be discovered, Had thrown aside these bloody witnesses.

Mérope: What hast thou told me? O these trembling hands Did on Cresphontes put that very armor When first he went to battle. Ye dear relics, O to what hands were ye delivered! monster, To seize this sacred armor.

Euricles: 'Tis the same Ægisthus did bring hither.

Mérope: Now behold it Stained with his blood! but in Alcides' temple Did they not see a poor old man?

Euricles: 'Twas Narbas: So Poliphontes owns.

Mérope: O dreadful truth! The villain, to conceal his crime, hath cast His body to the waves, and buried him In the rude ocean: O I see it all, All my sad fate: O my unhappy son!

Euricles: Would you not have the traitor brought before you, And questioned here?

SCENE VI.

Mérope, Euricles, Ismenia, Erox, Guards.

Erox: Permit me in the name Of Poliphontes, my rejected master. Perhaps rejected but because unknown, To offer you, in this distressful hour, His best assistance: he already knows Ægisthus is no more, and bears a part In your misfortunes.

Mérope: That I know he does, A joyful part, and reaps the fruits of them, The throne of my Cresphontes, and Ægisthus.

Erox: That throne he wishes but to share with you, And throw his sceptre at thy feet; the crown He hopes will make him worthy of thy hand: But to my hands the murderer must be given, For sacred is the power of punishment, 'Tis a king's duty; he alone must wield The sword of justice, the throne's best support, That to his people and to you he owes; Midst hymen rites the murderer's blood shall flow, A great sacrifice.

Mérope: My hand alone Shall strike the fatal blow: though Poliphontes Reigns o'er Messene, he must leave to me The work of vengeance: let him keep my kingdom, But yield to me the right of punishment: On that condition, and on that alone, I will be his: go, and prepare the rites: This hand, fresh bleeding from the traitor's bosom, Shall at the altar join with Poliphontes

Erox: Doubtless, the king, whose sympathetic heart Feels for your woes, will readily consent.

SCENE VII.

Mérope, Euricles, Ismenia.

Mérope: O Euricles, this vile detested marriage. Whate'er I promised, ne'er will come to pass: This arm shall pierce the savage murderer's breast, And instant turn the dagger to my own.

Euricles: O! madam, let me by the gods conjure you—

Mérope: They have oppressed me sorely; I have been Too long the object of their wrath divine: They have deprived me of my dearest child, And at their altars shall I ask a husband? Shall I conduct a stranger to the throne Of my forefathers? Wouldst thou have me join The hymeneal to the funeral torch? Shall Mérope still raise her weeping eyes To heaven, that shines no more on my Ægisthus? Shall she wear out her melancholy days Beneath a hateful tyrant, and expect In tears and anguish an old age of sorrow? When all is lost, and not even hope remains, To live is shameful, and to die, our duty.

ACT III.

SCENE I.

Narbas: O grief! O horror! O the weight of age! The youthful hero's warm imprudent ardor Was not to be restrained; his courage burst The inglorious chains of vile obscurity, And he is lost to me, perhaps forever. How shall I dare to see my royal mistress! Unhappy Narbas! hither art thou come Without Ægisthus; Poliphontes reigns, That subtle, proud artificer of fraud, That savage murderer, who pursued us still From clime to clime, and laid the snares of death On every side, fixed on the sacred throne, Which by his crimes so oft he hath profaned, The proud usurper sits, and smiles secure: Hide me, ye gods, from his all-piercing eye, And save Ægisthus from the tyrant's sword: O guide me, heaven, to his unhappy mother, And let me perish at her feet! Once more I see the palace, where the best of kings Was basely slain, and his defenceless child Saved in these arms; and after fifteen years Shall I return to fill a mother's heart With anguish? Who will lead me to the queen? No friend appears to guide me: but behold, Near yonder tomb I see a weeping crowd, And hear their loud laments! Within these walls Forever dwells some persecuting god.

SCENE II.

Narbas, Ismenia.

[At the farther end of the stage several of the queen's attendants, near the tomb of Cresphontes.]

Ismenia: What bold intruder presses thus unknown To the queen's presence, and disturbs the peace Of her retirement? comes he from the tyrant, A spy upon our griefs, to count the tears Of the afflicted?

Narbas: Whosoe'er thou art, Excuse the boldness of a poor old man; Forgive the intrusion; I would see the queen, Perhaps may serve her.

Ismenia: What a time is this Which thou hast chosen to interrupt her griefs! Respect a mother's bitter sorrows; hence, Unhappy stranger, nor offend her sight.

Narbas: O, in the name of the avenging gods, Have pity on my age, my misfortunes: I am no stranger here: O, if you serve And love the queen, forgive the tears that long Have flowed for her, and trust a heart that feels For Mérope as deeply as thy own. What tomb is that where you so late did join Your griefs?

Ismenia: The tomb of an illustrious hero, A wretched father, and a hapless king, The tomb of great Cresphontes.

Narbas: [Going towards the tomb My loved master!] Ye honored ashes!

Ismenia: But Cresphontes' wife Is more to be lamented still.

Narbas: What worse Could happen to her?

Ismenia: A most dreadful stroke; Her son is slain.

Narbas: Her son! Ægisthus! gods! And is Ægisthus dead?

Ismenia: All know it here Too well

Narbas: Her son?

Ismenia: A barbarous assassin Did slay him at Messene's gates.

Narbas: O death, I did foretell thee: horror and despair! Is the queen sure, and art thou not deceived?

Ismenia: O 'tis too plain; we have undoubted proofs; It must be so: he is no more.

Narbas: Is this The fruit of all my care?

Ismenia: The wretched queen, Abandoned to despair, will scarce survive him: She lived but for her child, and now the ties Are loosed that bound her to this hated life: But, ere she dies, with her own hand she waits To pierce the murderer's heart, and be revenged; Ev'n at Cresphontes' tomb his blood shall flow. Soon will the victim, by the king's permission, Be hither brought, to perish at her feet: But Mérope is lost in grief, and therefore Would wish to be alone: you must retire.

Narbas: If it be so, why should I seek the queen? I will but visit yonder tomb, and die.

SCENE III.

Ismenia: [Alone.] This old man seems most worthy: how he wept! Whilst the unfeeling slaves around us seem, Like their proud master, but to mock our sorrows: What interest could he have? yet tranquil pity Doth seldom shed so many tears; methought He mourned the lost Ægisthus like a father: He must be sought—but here's a dreadful sight.

SCENE IV.

Mérope, Ismenia, Euricles, Ægisthusin Chains, Guards, Sacrificers.

Mérope: [Near the tomb.] Bring forth that horrid victim to my sight; I must invent some new unheard of torment, That may be equal to his crime; alas! Not to my grief, that were impossible.

Ægisthusin: Dear have I bought thy momentary kindness, Guardians of innocence, protect me now!

Euricles: Before the traitor suffers, let him name His vile accomplices.

Mérope: [Coming forward.] He must; he shall: Say, monster, what induced thee to a crime So horrible to nature! How had I E'er injured thee?

Ægisthusin: Now bear me witness, gods, You who avenge the perjuries of men, If e'er my lips knew fraud or base imposture; I told thee naught but simple truth: thy heart, Fierce as it was, relented at my tale, And you stretched forth a kind, protecting hand; So soon is justice weary of her talk? Unwitting I have shed some precious blood: Whose was it, tell me, what new interest sways thee?

Mérope: What interest? barbarian!

Ægisthusin: O'er her cheek A deadly paleness spreads: it wounds my soul To see her thus. O I would spill my blood A thousand times to save her.

Mérope: Subtle villain! How artfully dissembled is that grief! He kills me, and yet seems to weep my fate. [She falls back into the arms of Ismenia.]

Euricles: Madam, avenge yourself, avenge the laws, The cause of nature, and the blood of kings.

Ægisthusin: Is this the royal justice of a court? Ye praise and flatter first, and then condemn me. Why did I leave my peaceful solitude! O good old man, what will thy sorrows be, And thou, unhappy mother, whose dear voice So oft foretold—

Mérope: Barbarian, and hast thou A mother? I had been a mother yet But for thy rage, thou hast destroyed my son.

Ægisthusin: If I am thus unhappy, if he was Indeed thy son, I ought to suffer for it; But though my hand was guilty, yet my heart Was innocent: heaven knows I would have given This day my life to save or his or thine.

Mérope: Didst thou take this armor from him?

Ægisthusin: No: It is my own.

Mérope: What sayest thou?

Ægisthusin: Yes; I swear By thee, by him, by all thy ancestors, My father gave to me that precious gift.

Mérope: Thy father! where? in Elis: how he moves me! What was his name? speak, answer.

Ægisthusin: Polycletes: I've told thee so already.

Mérope: O thou rivest My heart: what foolish pity stopped my vengeance? It is too much: assist me, friends, bring here The monster, the perfidious— [Lifting up the dagger.] O ye manes Of my dear son, this bloody arm—

Narbas: [Entering on a sudden.] O gods! What wouldst thou do?

Mérope: Who calls?

Narbas: Stop: stop—alas! If I but name his mother, he's undone.

Mérope: Die, traitor.

Narbas: Stop.

Ægisthusin: [Turning towards Narbas.] My father!

Mérope: Ha! his father!

Ægisthusin: [To Narbas.] What do I see? and whither wert thou going? Camest thou to be a witness of my death?

Narbas: O, madam, go no further: Euricles, Remove the victim, let me speak to thee.

Euricles: [Takes away Ægisthus, and shuts up the lower part of the scene.] O heaven!

Mérope: [Coming forward.] Thou makest me tremble: I was going To avenge my son.

Narbas: [Kneeling down.] To sacrifice—Ægisthus.

Mérope: Ægisthus! ha!

Narbas: 'Twas he, whom thy rash arm Had well nigh slain; believe me, 'twas Ægisthus.

Mérope: And lives he then?

Narbas: 'Tis he, it is your son.

Mérope: [Fainting in the arms of Ismenia.] I die!

Ismenia: Good heaven!

Narbas: [To Ismenia.] Recall her fleeting spirit; This sudden transport of tumultuous joy, Mixed with anxiety and tender fears, May quite o'erpower her.

Mérope: [Coming to herself.] Narbas, is it you? Or do I dream? is it my son? where is he? Let him come hither.

Narbas: No: refrain your love, Restrain your tenderness. [To Ismenia.] O keep the secret; The safety of the queen, and of Ægisthus, Depend on that.

Mérope: Alas! and must fresh danger Embitter my new joys? O dear Ægisthus, What cruel god still keeps thee from thy mother? Was he restored but to afflict me more?

Narbas: You knew him not, and would have slain your son: If his arrival here be once discovered, And you acknowledge him, he's lost forever. Dissemble, therefore, for thou knowest that guilt Reigns in Messene: thou art watched; be cautious.

SCENE V.

Mérope, Euricles, Narbas, Ismenia.

Euricles: 'Tis the king's order, madam, that we seize—

Mérope: Whom?

Euricles: The young stranger, whom thou had'st condemned To death.

Mérope: [With transport.] That stranger is my child, my son: They would destroy him, Narbas, let us fly—

Narbas: No: stay.

Mérope: It is my son; they'll have him from me, My dear Ægisthus: why is this?

Euricles: The king Would question him before he dies.

Mérope: Indeed! And knows he then I am his mother?

Euricles: No: 'Tis yet a secret to them all.

Mérope: We'll fly To Poliphontes, and implore his aid.

Narbas: Fear Poliphontes, and implore the gods.

Euricles: Howe'er Ægisthus may alarm the tyrant, Thy promised nupitals make his pardon sure: Bound to each other in eternal bonds, Thy son will soon be his; though jealousy May now subsist, it must be lost in love When he's your husband.

Narbas: He your husband, gods! I'm thunderstruck.

Mérope: I will no longer bear Such anguish, let me hence.

Narbas: Thou shalt not go: Unhappy mother! thou shalt ne'er submit To these detested nuptials.

Euricles: She is forced To wed him, that she may avenge Cresphontes.

Narbas: He was his murderer.

Mérope: He! that traitor!

Narbas: Yes: By Poliphontes thy Ægisthus fell, His father, and his brothers: I beheld The tyrant weltering in Cresphontes' blood.

Mérope: O gods!

Narbas: I saw him glorying in his crimes; Saw him admit the foe, and through the palace Spread fire and slaughter; yet appeared to those Who knew him not, the avenger of that king Whom he had slain: I pierced the savage crowd, And in my feeble arms upraised your son, And bore him thence; the pitying gods protected His helpless innocence: these fifteen years, From place to place I led him, changed my name To Polycletes, hid him from the foe, And now at last it seems have brought him hither, To see a tyrant on Messene's throne, And Mérope the wife of Poliphontes.

Mérope: Thy tale has harrowed up my soul.

Euricles: He comes: 'Tis Poliphontes.

Mérope: Is it possible? Away, good Narbas, hide thee from his rage.

Narbas: Now, if Ægisthus e'er was dear to thee, Dissemble with the tyrant.

Euricles: We must hide This secret in the bottom of our hearts, A word may ruin all.

Mérope: [To Euricles.] Go thou and guard That precious treasure well.

Euricles: O doubt it not.

Mérope: My hopes depend on thee: he is my son Remember, and thy king.—The monster comes.

SCENE VI.

Mérope, Poliphontes, Erox, Ismenia, Attendants.

Euricles: The altar is prepared, the throne awaits you, Our interests soon will with our hearts be joined: As king, and husband, 'tis my duty now Both to defend and to avenge you, madam: Two of the traitors I have seized already, Who shall repay the murder with their blood: But, spite of all my care, the tardy vengeance Hath seconded but ill my purposes: You told me you would wish yourself to slay The murderer, and I gave him to your justice.

Mérope: O that I might be my own great avenger!

Euricles: 'Tis a king's duty, and shall be my care.

Mérope: Thine, saidst thou?

Euricles: Wherefore is the sacrifice Delayed? dost thou no longer love thy son?

Mérope: May all his foes meet with their due reward! But if this murderer has accomplices, By him perhaps I may hereafter learn Who killed my dear Cresphontes: they who slew The father would forever persecute The mother and the son: O if I e'er—

Euricles: I too could wish to be informed of that, And therefore I have taken him to my care.

Mérope: To thine?

Euricles: Yes, madam, and I hope to draw The secret from him.

Mérope: But you must not keep This murderer: I must have him; nay, you promised, You know you did— [Aside.] O cruel fate! my son! What art thou doomed to? [To Poliphontes.] Pity me, my lord!

Euricles: Whence is this sudden transport? he shall die.

Mérope: Who? he?

Euricles: His death shall satisfy thy soul.

Mérope: Ay: but I want to see, to speak to him.

Euricles: These starts of passion, and these sudden transports Of rage and tenderness, that face of horror, Might give me cause perhaps of just suspicion; And, to be plain with you, some strange disgust, Some groundless fears, some new alarm, hath raised This tempest in your soul; what have you heard From that old man who went so lately hence? Why doth he shun me? what am I to think? Who is he?

Mérope: O my lord! so lately crowned Do fears and jealousies already wait Around your throne?

Euricles: Why wilt not thou partake it? Then should I bid adieu to all my fears: The altar waits, prepared for Mérope And Poliphontes.

Mérope: Thou hast gained the throne, The gods have given it thee, and now thou wantest Cresphontes' wife to make his kingdom sure. This crime alone—

Ismenia: O stop—

Mérope: My lord, forgive me; I am a wretched mother; I have lost My all; the gods, the cruel gods have robbed me Of every bliss: O give me, give me back The murderer of my son!

Euricles: This hand shall shed The traitor's blood: come, madam, follow me.

Mérope: O gracious heaven! in pity to my woes, Preserve a mother, and conceal her weakness!

ACT IV.

SCENE I.

Euricles: I almost thought she had discovered something Touching her husband's murder, for she frowned Indignant on me; but I want her hand, And not her heart; the crowd will have it so; We must not disoblige them; by this marriage I shall secure them both: I look on her But as a slave that's useful to my purpose, Chained to my chariot wheels to grace my triumph, And little heed her hatred or her love. But thou hast talked to this young murderer, What thinkest thou of him?

Erox: He's immovable, Simple in speech, but of undaunted courage, He braves his fate: I little thought to find In one of his low birth a soul so great; I own, my lord, I cannot but admire him.

Euricles: Who is he?

Erox: That I know not; but most certain He is not one of those whom we employed To watch for Narbas.

Euricles: Art thou sure of that? The leader of that band I have myself Despatched, and prudent buried in his blood The dangerous secret; but this young unknown Alarms me: is it certain he destroyed Ægisthus? has propitious fate, that still Prevented all my wishes, been thus kind?

Erox: Mérope's tears, her sorrow, and despair, Are the best proofs; but all I see confirms Thy happiness, and fortune hath done more Than all our cares.

Euricles: Fortune doth often reach What wisdom cannot: but I know too well My danger, and the number of my foes, To leave that fortune to decide my fate: Whoe'er this stranger be, he must not live, His death shall purchase me this haughty queen, And make the crown sit firmer on my head. The people then, subjected to my power, Will think at last their prince is dead, and know That I avenged him: but, inform me, who Is this old man that shuns me thus? there seems Some mystery in his conduct; Mérope, Thou tellest me, would have slain the murderer, But that this old man did prevent her; what Could move him to it?

Erox: He's the young man's father, And came to implore his pardon.

Euricles: Ha! his pardon! I'll see, and talk with him; but he avoids me, And therefore I suspect him; but I'll know This secret: what could be the queen's strange purpose, In thus deferring what so ardently She seemed to wish for? all her rage was changed To tenderest pity: through her griefs methought A ray of joy broke forth.

Erox: What is her joy, Her pity, or her vengeance, now to thee?

Euricles: It doth concern me nearly; I have cause For many fears; but she approaches:—bring That stranger to me.

SCENE II.

Poliphontes, Erox, Ægisthus, Euricles, Mérope, Ismenia, Guards.

Mérope: Fulfil your word, sir, and avenge me; give The victim to my hands, and mine alone.

Euricles: You see I mean to keep it: he's before you: Revenge yourself, and shed the traitor's blood; Then, madam, with your leave, we'll to the altar.

Mérope: O gods!

Ægisthusin: [To Poliphontes.] Am I then to be made the purchase Of the queen's favor? my poor life indeed Is but of little moment, and I die Contented; but I am a stranger here, A helpless, innocent, unhappy stranger; If heaven has made thee king, thou shouldst protect me: I've slain a man, 'twas in my own defence; The queen demands my life; she is a mother, Therefore I pity her, and bless the hand Raised to destroy me: I accuse none here But thee, thou tyrant.

Euricles: Hence, abandoned villain; Darest thou insult—

Mérope: O pardon his rash youth, Brought up in solitude, and far removed From courts, he knows not the respect that's due To majesty.

Euricles: Amazing! justified By you!

Mérope: By me, my lord?

Euricles: Yes, madam, you. Is this the murderer of your son?

Mérope: My child, My son, the last of a long line of kings, Beneath a vile assassin's hand—

Ismenia: O heaven! What wouldst thou do?

Euricles: Thine eyes are fixed upon him With tenderness and joy; thy tears too flow, Though thou wouldst hide them from me.

Mérope: No: 'tis false: I would not, cannot hide them: well thou knowest I've too much cause to weep.

Euricles: Dry up your tears; He dies this moment: soldiers, do your office.

Mérope: [Coming forward.] O spare him, spare him.

Ægisthusin: Ha! she pities me.

Euricles: Despatch him.

Mérope: O he is—

Euricles: Strike.

Mérope: Stay, barbarian, He is—my son.

Ægisthusin: Am I thy son?

Mérope: [Embracing him.] Thou art: And heaven, that snatched thee from this wretched bosom, Which now too late hath opened my longing eyes, Restores thee to a weeping mother's arms But to destroy us both.

Ægisthusin: What miracle Is this, ye gods?

Euricles: A vile imposture: thou His mother? thou, who didst demand his death?

Ægisthusin: O if I die the son of Mérope I die contented, and absolve my fate.

Mérope: I am thy mother, and my love of thee Betrayed us both; we are undone, Ægisthus; Yes, Poliphontes, the important secret At length is thine; before thee stands my son, Cresphontes' heir; thy master, and thy king; The offspring of the gods, thy captive now; I have deceived thee, and I glory in it; 'Twas for my child: but nature has no power O'er tyrants' hearts, that still rejoice in blood: I tell thee, 'tis my son, 'tis my Ægisthus.

Euricles: Ha! can it be?

Ægisthusin: It is; it must be so; Her tears confirm it: yes, I am the son Of Mérope, my heart assures me of it: And, hadst thou not disarmed me, with this hand I would chastise thee, traitor.

Euricles: 'Tis too much; I'll bear no more: away with him.

Mérope: [Falling on her knees.] Behold Thus low on earth the wretched Mérope Falls at your feet, and bathes them with her tears: Doth not this humble posture speak my griefs, And say I am a mother? O I tremble When I look back on the dire precipice I have escaped, the murder of my son; Still I lament the involuntary crime Didst thou not say thou wouldst protect his youth, And be a father to him? and yet now Thou wouldst destroy him: O have pity on him: Some guilty hand bereaved him of a father; O save the son, defend the royal race, The seed of gods: defenceless and alone He stands before thee: trample not on him, Who is unable to resist thy power; Let him but live, and I am satisfied; Save but my child, and all shall be forgotten: O he would make me happy even in woe; My husband and my children all would live Once more in my Ægisthus:

O behold, His royal ancestors with me implore thee To spare the noble youth, and save thy king.

Ægisthusin: Rise, madam, rise, or I shall never believe Cresphontes was my father; 'tis beneath His queen, beneath the mother of Ægisthus To supplicate a tyrant; my fierce heart Will never stoop so low: undaunted long I braved the meanness of my former fortune, Nor am I dazzled by the splendid lustre Of these new honors; but I feel myself Of royal blood, and know I am thy son. Great Hercules, like me, began his days In misery and sorrow; but the gods Conducted him to immortality, Because, like me, he rose superior to them: To me his blood descends; O let me add His courage, and his virtues; let me die Worthy of thee; be that my heritage! Cease then thy prayers, nor thus disgrace the blood Of those immortal powers from whom I sprang.

Euricles: [To Mérope.] Trust me, I bear a part in your misfortunes, Feel for your griefs, and pity your distress; I love his courage, and esteem his virtue; He seems well worthy of the royal birth Which he assumes; but truths of such importance Demand more ample proofs; I take him therefore Beneath my care, and, if he is thy son, I shall adopt him mine.

Ægisthusin: Thou, thou adopt me?

Mérope: Alas! my child!

Euricles: His fate depends on thee: It is not long since, to secure his death. Thou didst consent to marry Poliphontes; Now thou wouldst save him, shall not love do more Than vengeance?

Mérope: Ha! barbarian!

Euricles: Madam, know His life, or death, depends on thy resolve: I know your love, your tenderness, too well, To think you will expose to my just wrath So dear an object by a harsh refusal.

Mérope: My lord, at least let me be free, and deign—

Euricles: He is your son, or he's a traitor, madam; I must be yours before I can protect him, Or be revenged on both; a word from you Decides his fate, or punishment, or pardon; Or as his mother I shall look upon you As his accomplice; therefore make your choice: I will receive your answer at the temple Before the attesting gods. [To the soldiers.] Guard well your prisoner: Come, follow me: [Turning to Mérope.] I shall expect you, madam; Be quick in your resolve; confirm his birth By giving me your hand; your answer only Saves or condemns him; and as you determine He is my victim, madam, or—my son.

Mérope: O grant me but the pleasure to behold him; Restore him to my love, to my despair.

Euricles: You'll see him at the temple.

Ægisthusin: [As the guards are carrying him off.] O great queen, I dare not call thee by the sacred name Of mother, do not, I beseech thee, aught Unworthy of thyself, or of Ægisthus; For, if I am thy son, thy son shall die As a king ought.

SCENE III.

Mérope: [Alone.] Ye cruel spoilers, why Will you thus tear him from me? O he's gone, I've lost him now forever; wherefore, heaven, Didst thou restore him to a mother's vows, Or why preserve him in a foreign land, To fall at last a wretched sacrifice, A victim to the murderer of his father? O save him, hide him in the desert's gloom; Direct his steps, and shield him from the tyrant!

SCENE IV.

mérope, narbas, **Euricles:** Mérope, O Narbas, knowest thou the unhappy fate To which I am doomed?

Narbas: Well I know the king Must die; I know Ægisthus is in chains.

Mérope: And I destroyed him.

Narbas: You?

Mérope: Discovered all: But thinkest thou, Narbas, ever mother yet Could see a child, as I did, and be silent? But it is past: and now I must repair My weakness with my crimes.

Narbas: What crimes?

SCENE V.

Mérope, Narbas, Euricles, Ismenia.

Ismenia: O madam, Now call forth all the vigor of your soul, The hour of trial comes: the fickle crowd, Still fond of novelty, with ardent zeal, Press forward to behold the expected nuptials; Each circumstance conspires to serve the tyrant: Already the bribed priest has made his god Declare for Poliphontes: "He received Your vows, Messene was a witness to them, And heaven will see the contract is fulfilled:" Thus spoke the holy seer; the people answered With acclamations loud, and songs of joy; They little know the grief that wrings thy heart; But thank the gods for these detested nuptials, And bless the tyrant for his cruelty.

Mérope: And are my sorrows made the public joy?

Narbas: O these are dreadful means to save thy son.

Mérope: They are indeed: thou shudderest at the thought: It is a crime.

Narbas: But to destroy thy child Were still more horrible.

Mérope: Away: despair Has given me courage, and restored my virtue: Let's to the temple; there I'll show the people My dear Ægisthus; 'twixt myself and the altar Will place my son; the gods will see him there; They will defend him, for from them he sprang: Too long already persecuting heaven Hath scourged his helpless innocence; and now It will avenge him: O I will set forth His savage murderer in the blackest colors, Till vengeance shall inspire each honest heart With tenfold rage: now dread a mother's cries, Ye cruel tyrants, for they will be heard: They come; alas! I tremble yet, despair And horror seize me: hark, they call, my son Is dying: see the cruel murderer plants A dagger in his breast: a moment more And he is lost: ye savage ministers [Turning to the sacrificers.] Of the base tyrant, you must drag the victim Up to the altar; can you, must you do it? O vengeance, duty, tenderness, and love, And thou great nature, what will ye ordain, What will ye do with an unhappy queen, Abandoned to despair?

ACT V.

SCENE I.

Ægisthus, Narbas, Euricles.

Narbas: Our fate is yet uncertain, whilst the tyrant Still keeps us in the palace; all my fears Are for Ægisthus: O my king, my son, Let me still call thee by that tender name, O live, disarm the tyrant's rage, preserve A life so dear, so precious to Messene, So valued by thy faithful Narbas!

Euricles: Think On the poor queen, who, for thy sake alone A humble suppliant, sprinkles with her tears The tyrant's murderous hand.

Ægisthusin: I'm scarce awakened From my long dream, I seem as one new-born; A wandering stranger in a world unknown; New thoughts inspire, new day breaks in upon me; The son of Mérope, and great Cresphontes; And yet his murderer triumphs; he commands, And I obey; the blood of Hercules A captive and in chains!

Narbas: O would to heaven The grandson of Alcides still remained Unknown in Elis!

Ægisthusin: Is it not most strange, Young as I am, that I should know already, By sad experience, every human woe? Horror and shame, and banishment, and death, Since my first dawn of life, have pressed upon me: A persecuted wretch I wandered long From clime to clime, hid in the desert's gloom, I languished there in vile obscurity: Yet, bear me witness, heaven, midst all my woes Nor murmured nor complained: though proud ambition Devoured my soul, I learned the humble virtues That suited best my hard and low condition: Still I respected, still obeyed thee, Narbas, And loved thee as a father; nor would e'er Have wished to find another, but high heaven Would change my fate to make me but more wretched: I am Cresphontes' son, yet can't avenge him; I've found a mother, and a tyrant now Will snatch her from me; soon she must be his: O I could curse the hour that gave me birth, And the kind succor which thy goodness lent me: O why didst thou hold back the uplifted hand Of a mistaken mother? But for thee I had fulfilled my fate, and all my woes Had ended with my life.

Narbas: We are undone, The tyrant comes.

SCENE II.

poliphontes, ægisthus, narbas, euricles, Guards.

Euricles: [To Narbas and the rest.] Retire: and thou, rash youth, Whose tender years demand my pity, list, And mark me well; for the last time I come To give thee here thy choice of life or death, Thy present and thy future happiness, Thy very being hangs upon my will: I can advance thee to the highest rank, Or shut thee in a dungeon, kill or save thee: Removed from courts, and bred in solitude, Thou art not fit to govern; let me guide In wisdom's ways thy inexperienced youth; Assume not in thy humble state a pride Which thou mistakest for virtue: if thy birth Be mean and lowly, bend to thy condition; If happier fate hath given thee to descend From royal blood, and thou wert born a prince, Make thyself worthy of thy noble rank, And learn of me to rule: the queen, thou seest, Has set thee an example; she obeys, And meets me at the temple; follow her, Tread in my steps, attend us to the altar, And swear eternal homage to thy king, To Poliphontes: if thou fearest the gods, Call them to witness thy obedience; haste, The gates of glory open to receive, And not to enter may be fatal to thee: Determine therefore now, and answer me.

Ægisthusin: How can I answer when thou hast disarmed me? Thy words, I own, astonish and confound; But give me back that weapon which thy fears Have wrested from me; give me my good sword, And I will answer as I ought; will show thee, Perfidious as thou art, which is the slave, And which the master, whether Poliphontes Was born to rule o'er princes, or Ægisthus To scourge oppressors.

Euricles: Impotence and rashness! My kind indulgence makes thee insolent: Thou thinkest I'll not demean myself so far To punish an unknown rebellious slave; But mercy, thus abused, will change to wrath: I give thee but a moment to determine, And shall expect thee at the altar; there To die or to obey: guards, bring him to me: Narbas, to you and Euricles I leave The haughty rebel; you shall answer for him: I know your hatred of me, and I know Your weakness, too, but trust to your experience, You will advise him for the best; meantime Remember, whether he's the son of Narbas Or Mérope, he must obey, or die.

SCENE III.

Ægisthus, Narbas, Euricles.

Ægisthusin: I'll listen to no counsel but the voice Of vengeance; O inspire me, Hercules, O from thy seat of endless bliss look down On thy Ægisthus, animate his soul, And guide his footsteps! Poliphontes calls, I will attend him; let us to the altar.

Narbas: Wilt thou then die?

Euricles: We must not follow thee: Let us collect our few remaining friends, And strive—

Ægisthusin: Away: another time my soul Would listen to your kind advice, for well I know ye love me; but no counsellors Must now be heard save all-directing heaven And my own heart: the irresolute alone Is swayed by others, but the blood of heroes Will guide itself: away, the die is cast. What do I see? O gracious heaven! my mother!

SCENE IV.

Mérope, Ægisthus, Narbas, Euricles, Attendants.

Mérope: Once more, Ægisthus, by the tyrant's order, We meet together; he has sent me to thee: Think not that, after these detested nuptials, I mean to live; but for thy sake, my son, I have submitted to this shameful bondage: For thee alone I fear; for thee I bear This load of infamy: O live, Ægisthus, Let me entreat thee, live; ere thou canst rule Thou must obey, and servitude must open The path to vengeance; thou contemnest my weakness, I know thou dost; but O the more I love The more I fear. O my dear child—

Ægisthusin: Be bold, And follow me.

Mérope: Alas! what wouldst thou do? Why, ye just gods, why was he made too virtuous?

Ægisthusin: Seest thou my father's tomb? dost thou not hear His voice? art thou a mother and a queen? O if thou art, come on.

Mérope: Methinks some god Inspires thy soul, and raises thee above The race of mortals: now I see the blood Of great Alcides flows through every vein, And animates Ægisthus: O my son, Give me a portion of thy noble fire, And raise this drooping heart!

Ægisthusin: Hast thou no friends Within this fatal temple?

Mérope: Once I had A crowd of followers when I was a queen, But now their virtue sinks beneath the weight Of my misfortunes, and they bend their necks To this new yoke: they hate the tyrant, yet Have crowned him; love their queen, and yet desert her.

Ægisthusin: By all art thou abandoned; at the altar Waits Poliphontes for thee?

Mérope: Yes.

Ægisthusin: His soldiers, Do they attend him?

Mérope: No: he is surrounded By that ungrateful faithless crowd that once Encircled Mérope, by them upled To the altar, I will force for thee alone A passage.

Ægisthusin: And alone I'll follow thee: There shall I meet my ancestors divine; The gods who punish murderers will be there.

Mérope: Alas! these fifteen years they have contemned thee.

Ægisthusin: They did it but to try me.

Mérope: What's thy purpose?

Ægisthus in: No matter what; let us begone: farewell My mournful friends, at least ye soon shall know The son of Mérope deserved your care. [To Narbas, embracing him.] Narbas, believe me, thou shalt never blush To own me for thy son.

SCENE V.

Narbas: What means Ægisthus? Alas! my cares are fruitless all and vain: I hoped the sure slow-moving hand of time Would justify the ways of heaven, and place The wronged Ægisthus on Messene's throne; But guilt still triumphs, and my hopes are vanished; His courage will destroy him; death awaits His disobedience. [A noise within.]

Euricles: Hark! they shout.

Narbas: Alas! It is the fatal signal.

Euricles: Let us listen.

Narbas: I tremble.

Euricles: Doubtless, at the very moment When Poliphontes was to wed the queen, She has dissolved the shameful bonds by death, For so her rage had purposed.

Narbas: Then Ægisthus Must perish too, she should have lived for him.

Euricles: The noise increases, like the rolling thunder Onward it comes, and every moment grows More dreadful.

Narbas: Hark! I hear on every side The trumpets sound, the groans of dying men, And clash of swords; they force the palace.

Euricles: See Yon bloody squadron; look, it is dispersed; They fly.

Narbas: Perhaps to serve the tyrant's cause.

Euricles: Far as my eyes can reach I see them still Engaged in fight.

Narbas: Whose blood will there be shed? Surely I heard the name of Mérope, And of Ægisthus.

Euricles: Thanks to heaven, the ways Are open, I will hence, and know my fate. [He goes out.]

Narbas: I'll follow thee, but not with equal steps, For I am old and feeble: O ye gods! Restore my strength, give to this nerveless arm Its former vigor; let me save my king, Or yield up the poor remnant of my days, And die in his defence.

SCENE VI.

Narbas, Ismenia.

[A crowd of people.]

Narbas: Who's there? Ismenia? Bloody and pale! O horrid spectacle! Art thou indeed Ismenia?

Ismenia: O my voice, My breath is lost; let me recover them, And I will tell thee all.

Narbas: My son— The queen—do they yet live?

Ismenia: I'm scarce myself; Half dead with fear; the crowd has borne me hither.

Narbas: How does Ægisthus?

Ismenia: O he is indeed The son of gods; a stroke so terrible, So noble! never did the unconquered courage Of great Alcides with a deed so bold Astonish mortals.

Narbas: O my son, my king, The work of my own hands, the gallant hero!

Ismenia: Crowned with fresh flowers the victim was prepared, And Hymen's torches round the altar blazed, When Poliphontes, wrapped in gloomy silence, Stretched forth his eager hand; the priest pronounced The solemn words;

amidst her weeping maids Stood fixed in grief the wretched Mérope; Slow she advanced, and trembling in these arms, Instead of Hymen, called on death; the people Were silent all; when from the holy threshold, A more than mortal form, a youthful hero Stepped forth, and sudden darted to the altar; It was Ægisthus; there undaunted seized The axe that for the holy festival Had been prepared; then with the lightning's speed He ran, and felled the tyrant; "Die," he cried, "Usurper, die; now take your victim, gods." Erox, the monster's vile accomplice, saw His master weltering in his blood, upraised His hand for vengeance; but Ægisthus smote The slave, and laid him at the tyrant's feet: Meantime, recovered, Poliphontes rose And fought; I saw Ægisthus wounded; saw The fierce encounter: the guards ran to part them; When Mérope, such power has mighty love, Pierced through opposing multitudes, and cried, "Stop, ye inhuman murderers, 'tis my son, 'Tis my Ægisthus, turn your rage on me, And plant your daggers in the breast of her Who bore him, of his mother, and your queen:" Her shrieks alarmed the crowd, and a firm band Of faithful friends secured her from the rage Of the rude soldiers; then might you behold The broken altars, and the sacred ruins: On every side, confusion, war, and slaughter Triumphant reigned; brothers on brothers rose, Children were butchered in their mothers' arms, Friends murdered friends, the dying and the dead Together lay, and o'er their bodies trampled The flying crowd; with groans the temple rung. Amidst the uproar of contending legions I lost Ægisthus and the queen, and fled: In vain I asked each passing stranger whither They bent their way; their answers but increased My terrors; still they cry, he falls, he's dead, He conquers; all is darkness and confusion: I ran, I flew, and by the timely aid Of these kind friends have reached this place of safety: But still I know not whether yet the queen And great Ægisthus are preserved; my heart Is full of terrors.

Narbas: Thou great arbiter Of all that's mortal, providence divine, Complete thy glorious work, protect the good, Support the innocent, reward the wretched, Preserve my son, and I shall die in peace! Ha! midst you crowd do I behold the queen?

SCENE VII.

Mérope, Ismenia, Narbas, People, Soldiers.

[At the farther part of the stage is exposed the corpse of Poliphontes, covered with a bloody robe.]

Mérope: Priests, warriors, friends, my fellow-citizens, Attend, and hear me in the name of heaven. Once more I swear, Ægisthus is your king, The scourge of guilt, the avenger of his father, And yonder bleeding corpse, a hated monster, The foe of gods and men, who slew my husband, My dear Cresphontes, and his helpless children, Oppressed Messene, and usurped my kingdom, Yet dared to offer me his savage hand, Still reeking with the blood of half my race. [Meeting Ægisthus, who enters with the axe in his hand.] But here behold Messene's royal heir, My only hope, your queen's illustrious son, Who conquered Poliphontes: see, my friends, This good old man, [Pointing to Narbas.] Who saved him from the tyrant, And brought him here: the gods have done the rest.

Narbas: I call those gods to witness, 'tis your king; He fought for them, and they protected him.

Ægisthusin: O hear a mother pleading for her son, And know me for your king! I have avenged A father, I have conquered but for you.

Mérope: If still ye doubt, look on his glorious wounds: Who, but the great descendant of Alcides, Could save Messene thus, and scourge a tyrant? He will support his subjects, and avenge An injured people: hark! the voice of heaven Confirms your choice, and speaks to you in thunder; It cries aloud, "Ægisthus is my son."

SCENE VIII.

Mérope, Ægisthus, Ismenia, Narbas, Euricles, People.

Euricles: O madam, show yourself to the pleased people, The king's return has fixed their wavering minds, And every heart is ours: the impatient crowd Sheds tears of joy, and blesses your noble son: Forever will they hold this glorious day In sweet remembrance; ardently they long To see their youthful sovereign, to behold His faithful Narbas, and adore their queen: The name of Poliphontes is detested; Thine and the king's the praise of every tongue. O haste, enjoy thy victory and thy fame; Enjoy a nobler prize, thy people's love.

Ægisthusin: To heaven ascribe the glory, not to me; Thence comes our happiness, and thence our virtue: While Mérope survives, I will not mount

Messene's throne, my joy shall be to place A mother there; and thou, my dearest Narbas, Shall be my friend, my guide, my father still.

End

www.ingramcontent.com/pod-product-compliance
Lightning Source LLC
Chambersburg PA
CBHW031429040426
42444CB00006B/743